AF446118

TIES

IN

LOVE

by

EMMA MATEO

Copyright @ 2022 Emma Mateo

All rights reserved

TABLE OF CONTENTS

CHAPTER 1

I am not your average girl, I am not your average daughter, I am not your average sister, and I am not your average friend. I am different from everyone, and least almost everyone. My friend, Alice, she is just like me. Almost like my twin sister, only we don't look alike. She has blonde hair I have black hair; she has brown eyes I have blue eyes. But we like the same things. We are both interested in the afterlife and we both believe in ghosts. And we both agree that high school is the complete worst. We are our own group, nobody else. We like being in the library, quiet places.

Besides our looks, the only difference is I have an annoying younger brother and she is an only child. I wish she was my sister instead of having my brother. We walk to school; we don't drive or take the bus. Neither of us drive, that is one of the main cause of death and Alice doesn't like the bus because it's too noisy and crowded, neither do I.

Everybody who knows me knows my mom but everybody who knows my mom doesn't know me, but they do know my brother. I am completely different from the both of them, some even believe I am adopted or a maid. We do look the same but are nothing alike. My mother, brother, and I all look the same. Black hair, blue eyes. But I am nothing like them.

Alice is the only person who knows I am alive. Sometimes my mom will ask me to go with her and Dari to her work, and that's only never. But when I do go, I don't like it. I'd rather be at home, alone or with Alice.

My mom works as a personal assistant for the owner of

Walker Designs. It may look like I don't pay attention,

but I do.

Besides Alice, Mr. Walker is the only one who knows of

my existence. I found out the only reason why mom takes

me with her is because Mr. Walker wants to see me. He

is the only adult who likes me, let alone tolerates me.

Even then I show him little to no respect or emotion. I am

like that with everyone except Alice, because she

understands me on a different level.

My mom would talk about me to Mr. Walker, saying that

I was a pain. So he said that he would like to meet me.

She thought that was a mistake and I did as well. He still

met me and now he always wants to meet me. I don't

know what he likes about me. But I can tell the only reason why my mom would even go along with it is because she is in love with him, she will do anything he asks.

They have never had sex; he doesn't like her in that way. He always buys me nice things, expensive things. Things like clothes and books. He even buys me the right clothes in the right color, he knows me better than my own mom. He once bought me a book about talking to the dead, then I had to give him a little respect.

Mr. Walker has a son, Luka, and he goes to my school. Luka and my brother are best friends, they are like twins, only Dari is homosexual and Luka is pansexual. Mom never worries about them trying to have sex, after all Luka is seventeen and Dari is twelve. But I know the truth. They have had sex, multiple times. I caught them once in Dari's room. I won't say what they were doing, but I will say they were bare. After Luka went home and mom went to bed, Dari came into my room.

He begged me not to tell mom, I understood why. He was mom's angel and if she found out she would forbid him from seeing Luka. Whether I love him or loathe him, he is my brother. I was never going to tell her in the first place, it wasn't my business. The next day mom asked me to come to work with her. I did. I knew why. We went straight into Mr. Walker's office.

I always stayed in his office while they both worked. I was fine with it; it was quiet in there.

Mr. Walker greet mom with the usual nod and me with a smile. Sometimes I wish I got the nod instead. I knew mom was lonely. I knew mom wanted Mr. Walker to help create her second miracle. Then that child would replace me, the mistake.

"Hello Jade, how are you today?"

"I am fine."

"Good. what do I have on the schedule, Sarah?"

"You have a board meeting at three and a dinner meeting tonight at eight with Mr. Lee and Mr. Roberts."

"Alright. Jade would you like to stay in my office?" I nodded, I never said much, he knew that.

"Okay, please enjoy yourself while we are gone."

He placed his hand on my head and smiled. As they walked away my mother glared at me. She hated me. I always knew that. After a while she began to believe Mr.

Walker had feeling for me and not her. She was very angry, she beat me. I went to school with a black eye and bruises everywhere. She still hates me to this day and her beliefs are still there. I wait in Mr. Walker's office with Dari.

"Luka is coming over and I'm going with him to go hang out."

"Okay."

"Will you be okay?"

"What?

 "Will you be okay?"

"Yes."

My brother has never asked if I was okay, he has never talked to me much. I knew why. Mom told him not to as a little child, she said he would be like me if he was

anywhere near me. He was her angel and I was her

demon. He believed her.

"Look, Jade, I really need to tell you something."

I stared at him, that was my answer, he knew that.

"I'm sorry. Sorry for not standing up to mom and trying

to protect you." He was apologizing.

"You have kept all of my secrets, and I have done

nothing good for you."

I have caught them multiple times.

"From now on, I am defending you when mom tries to

hurt you."

"You won't be her angel anymore."

"I don't care; I think I'm as far from an angel as I can get."

"You're human."

"Yup, and so are you. Thank you sis."

That is one word that I have never heard come from his mouth, and I've heard many. He smiles at me. I know I should do something but I don't know what. I smile back. That is the first time I have smiled in a long time. He smiles even wider and even laughs. Luka opens the door wearing a confused look. Dari smiles at him and I return my face to normal.

"Hey babe. What's going on?"

"Oh nothing, just having a little sibling conversation."

He actually called me his sister.

"Great. Thanks for covering for us Jade."

Wait, does mom not know about this?

"Mom knows you're going out right?"

"Come on Jade, let him go."

"No, she doesn't. And neither does Mr. Walker. Please

don't tell them."

"Where are you going?"

"Nowhere."

"By the eastside river."

"Babe! Don't tell her everything!"

"I have to!"

"Why!"

"She is my sister!"

"What if she rats us out? Then we'll both get in trouble!"

"She won-"

"I won't tell anyone, just be back before nine."

"Why?"

"Mom and Mr. Walker will be back around nine."

"Okay, thanks sis!"

"Be careful."

"Will do!" Babe they are dating now. I know I have to start acting like a sister. He knows once Luka turns eighteen they can't date anymore; it would be illegal.

I wait a few hours. I stare at the wall, every second of those hours until I hear footsteps. I stare at the wall even when the door opens.

Luka and Dari come in, laughing. I avert my eyes to look at them. Dari sits next to me while Luka sits across. Luka leans in to kiss him but Dari pulls back and stares at me. I stare at him; he knows my answer. When I look away, I said no.

He leans in a kisses Luka. I don't look but I can see from the corner of my eye. When I see things, I remember everything. Luka pulls at Dari's waist until Dari is sitting on his lap. Dari wraps his arms around Luka's neck while Luka runs his hand under Dari's shirt.

"Stop."

"What? Why?"

"Don't worry about her, you know how your sister is."

"Wait, why should we stop? Is this making you uncomfortable?"

"Why do you care?"

"Because he's my sister."

"Seriously Dari?"

"Yes."

"Stop. Dari get off."

"Okay."

"No, Dari. What the hell, Jade?"

"Stop. be quiet."

Luka moves the chair back to the other side of the room and sits there. We wait in silence.

"What was that for?"

"Stop."

"Why?"

"Luka, please listen."

"Fine."

We wait in silence until the door opens. Mr. Walker and mom. Dari and Luka looked at me with eyes opened wide.

"When did you get here, Luka?"

"A few hours ago."

"Oh, okay. And how are you two?"

"I'm great!" I just stare. He nods. Luka gets up.

"Hey dad, I'm staying over at a friend's house."

"Alright." Luka leaves and mom speaks up.

"I should probably get Dari home."

"Alright, what about Jade?"

"She said she'll stay with her friend."

I never said that, but it's better staying with Alice then my own mom. But I know why she said that. She's mad at me. So nobody finds out she beats me, she sends me to Alice's house to prevent her from beating me.

"Alright, I'll take her."

"Are you sure? I don't want that to be trouble for you."

"No trouble at all!"

"Okay, let's go Dari."

"Okay. Bye Mr. Walker, bye Jade." I stare at him and he smiles.

I stare at the wall once again. Dari and mom leave. Mr. Walker gets up and walks over to me with a book in his hand. "I was thinking of you when I saw this and I thought you'd love it."

It was a book I have always wanted. One I could never get because it was too expensive. There are only 10 of these books in the world and now I've got one of them. I reach for the book and take it. The cover is made of leather. I should say something.

"Thank you, Mr. Walker."

"No problem sweetie."

He smiles and kisses my forehead. Sometimes he does that, mom never does. He grabbed his coat and looked at me again.

“You ready to go?”

CHAPTER 2

He took me to her house. Alice was outside. Mr. Walker got out of the car and so did I. he introduced himself to Alice and she nodded. He understood me so he understood her. He knocked on the door and Alice's mom answered.

"Oh my, to what do I owe this pleasure of meeting you, Mr. Walker?"

"I am here to drop off Jade, her mother said you knew she was coming."

"She what? Oh dear."

"Is there a problem?"

"Not at all. Thank you very much, Mr. Walker."

"Are you sure there is no problem? Did you not know she was coming?"

"Well, I did."

"You don't sound sure."

"I can assure you everything will be fine Mr. Walker. No need to worry, Jade always comes over and she is always welcome."

"How often does she come over?"

"More often than not. But after all, they are friends." I knew Mr. Walker was skeptical about leaving me here, but I was safe here. More than my own house. Mrs. Lee knew why my mom sent me to her house, she knew all the things my mom did to me. In a way, Mrs. Lee and my mom are alike. They are both different from Alice and I,

but Mrs. Lee doesn't think her daughter was a mistake.
She understands Alice. She won't tell anyone because of
Dari. It would ruin his life. I don't want her to tell anyone
either. Well, he left. I went inside and Mrs. Lee went to
her room.

Alice and I went to her room. Her room looked like mine,
all black with candles and books. We sat on her bed.
"Did your mom hit you again?"

"No, but she sent me here."

"Are you sure you don't want to make her a voodoo doll?
Then we could finally cause her some pain. Great
karma." "No, Dari is still there."

"Okay. what about turning her into a pig and cooking
her? All we have to do now is cook her."

"No."

"Okay. But when will it be okay?"

"Never. I want to do it as much as you do but I have to think about Dari."

"Alright. Should we try to connect with them now?"

"Yes."

For her birthday, her mom got her Ouija board. Ever since then we have used it to communicate with the dead. We were skeptical of whether or not it was real so we ask the ghosts personal questions, questions only our family members would know. Alice asked a question that only her grandmother knew and the ghost was correct.

We don't try the board with ghosts we don't know, just family members. Tonight we try to communicate with

Alice's cousin. He died in a car accident five years ago, he was eighteen. We place our fingertips on the pancetta and ask our first question.

"Marcus, is that you?"

The piece slides up right . . . yes.

"Do you remember how you died?" The piece moves across the letters . . . C-A-R A-C-C-I-D-E-N-T.

"What is our name?"

It moves again . . . J-A-D-E-A-L-I-C-E.

"Where are you?"

Again . . . H-O-M-E We continue you talk to him, it is him. After an hour we decide to go to bed. "Goodnight Marcus." The piece slides down the middle . . . good bye.

Minutes later, I am swallowed by darkness. I sleep

peacefully. Marcus was Alice's cousin, not like her. He was my friend. He liked me. He told me on his eighteenth birthday. He said he wanted me. He said he wanted to kiss me, to make me his. Alice was my friend, I said no. He didn't take no for an answer.

He was driving home from the store, getting food for his family. He didn't stop at the red light. He crashed into two other cars. The others survived, he didn't. Often Alice would let me take her Ouija board home with me. One day I was reading a book when the piece started moving on its own. J-A-D-E

"Yes? Who is it?"

"M-A-R-C-U-S"

"Marcus? What do you need?"

Y-O-U I was afraid of what that meant. At the time I was eleven years old and he was eighteen. There was no way I would ever like him. I have never liked anyone that way. He was a friend. Now that I am sixteen, he is twenty-three.

"You are too old and you are dead."

T-H-A-T C-A-N B-E F-I-X-E-D

"No, I'm not killing myself. Sorry."

W-H-Y

"I don't know, but no."

I S-T-I-L-L L-U-V Y-O-U at that point I knew it was him, he always spelled love L-UV. Even then the answer was still no.

"Good night Marcus."

Goodbye . . . He still tries to contact me, sometimes I don't answer. And sometimes he gets mad. I know he does because the board is thrown off the table. At those times he won't contact me for a while which means a few days. Then he apologizes. I get up to Alice waking me up. I look her in the eyes, she looks upset. I wonder what she is thinking.

I stare back at her and she turns around. She goes into her closet and picks an outfit to wear. Often we share clothes but today I wear a hoodie and jeans. We talk outside and see her mother and a police officer talking outside. I know she didn't tell him about my mother, that is her brother. Officer Lee is twenty-three years old. He is kind and funny. We walked outside and they both smile. Mr. Lee is taller than Mr. Walker by one inch.

Mr. Lee is just like Mrs. Lee. He is new to the force but loves it all the same. He is just like his sister, always smiling. She often pushes him to get a girlfriend but he always says he doesn't have time. I always call adults by Mr. or Mrs. and their last name but Mr. Lee doesn't like that, or at least when he's not working. He prefers Uncle Jacob; he even wants me to call him that.

"Good morning ladies!"

"Morning Uncle Jacob."

He stares at me, waiting for an answer. I'm not sure what to say. He is wearing his uniform but Alice called him Uncle Jacob.

"Good morning Uncle Jacob."

"There you go Jade! How are you beautiful young ladies?"

"Good."

"Great!" He gives us both hugs and kisses before he says good-bye. Mrs. Lee takes us to the store to buy a new book. We buy a book about the Black Death.

Throughout the entire day, we read it in her room. We read until her mom calls us. We walk outside and see my mom and Dari. Dari looks happy to see me but mom doesn't. She glares at me.

"Sarah, please, you need to stop doing this. Jade is welcome to come over but please don't let it be under these conditions."

"Shut up. Don't tell me how to raise my daughter."

"I'm not telling you how to raise your daughter, I'm just saying what you're doing to your daughter is wrong."

"I'm doing nothing wrong to her."

"I know you beat her Sarah."

"What? Why you little bitch."

"Sarah! You can't call your daughter that!" I've been called worse.

"You snitched!"

"No, she didn't. I knew."

"How?"

"When she went to school, she went to school with bruises on her arms. She isn't capable of doing that to herself and Dari would never hurt his sister but you, you

hate her."

"I never wanted her."

"Sarah! You can't say that!"

"Well why would I lie to her?"

"That isn't right!"

"She is nothing like Dari or me, what am I supposed to

do with her?"

"Care for her."

"No, I want nothing to do with her. You care for her.

She's your daughter now!"

"Mom!"

"What?"

"She's my sister! I don't want her to go!"

"She's nothing like us Dari, she doesn't deserve us!"

"No, you're wrong. We don't deserve her!"

"What?"

"She's special!"

"She's a mistake!"

"Mom! No she's not!"

"Hush Dari, go wait in the car."

"But!"

"Go!" Dari walked away, staring at me with sad eyes. He stood up for me, and that alone was enough.

"She can come pick up her stuff, but she's yours now, do what you want."

"Sarah, please reconsider."

"No, Diana I'm done with that brat!"

"Sarah."

She walks out the door and drives away. Mrs. Lee looks at me and runs over to hug me and Alice. I look at Alice as she looks at me, and for the first time in a long time, I see sorrow in her eyes. Alice and Mrs. Lee drive me to my house to pick up my stuff. I go inside and into my room. I gather all my books and some of my clothes.

I hear footsteps and turn around. Dari stands in the threshold of my door, with tears streaming down his face. I turn around and he walked up to me. He gives me a hug and cries into my shoulder. Unsure what to do, I hug him back and stroke his head.

"I'm sorry Jade. I'm so sorry."

"It's okay."

"Will you be okay?"

"Yes. Will you?"

"I'll be fine."

"Good."

"Will I see you at school?"

"Yes."

"Okay. I love you sis."

"I love you too."

I didn't even know what I was saying, it just came out.

I'm glad I said it. Dari left into his own room and I heard

footsteps growing louder. I turned again and saw my mother. She glared at me.

"I wish you were never born." No answer.

"You ruined my life!" No answer.

"You want to know why your father left?" That struck me hard. I never knew why my father left.

"He left because you were born. He left me! Then when Dari was born. I tried to show him I fixed your mistake but he stayed away. I even said I would get rid of you, he still stayed away."

If Dari knew this he would hate me for the rest of his life, just like mom.

"That's the reason why he left, it was all your fault! If you had never been born I would be happy. Dari is all I have and now he is angry with me because of you!" She threw her wine glass at my head and it shattered.

It stung a little. I've been hit worse.

"I hate you! You bitch! You whore! asshole! I wish you were never born you little shithead! I fucking hate you!" She threw her shoes at me and anything she could find.

She cussed me out until the only that she could do was hit me to her drunk heart's content. She ran up to me and slapped me down. When I was on the floor, she kicked me. She kicked me over and over again. I heard a nearby door open and saw Dari standing at the door.

"Mom! Stop! Leave her alone! Mom! MOM!"

"Go to bed Dari!"

"NO! Leave her alone!"

"NOW!"

"NO!" Dari grabbed her and threw her on the bed.

He grabbed my bag and picked me off the floor. Blood was dripping from my forehead and it felt like I had been stabbed ten times. He dragged me outside. Mrs. Lee and Alice ran out of the car to see if I was okay.

"What happened?"

"Nothing, just get her out of here."

"What happened?"

"Leave! Hurry!" They started to turn but I held onto Dari's hand.

"Come."

"I can't."

"She'll hurt you."

"I don't care."

"I do."

"Jade, you have to leave."

"Come."

"I-I . . . fine."

Dari helped me in the car and then Mrs. Lee drove away. I sat still, it hurt too much to move. I felt Dari lean into me, that hurt a lot. He laid his head on my lap, I knew he needed it no matter how much it hurt. I stroked his head gently. Soon after he fell asleep and so did I.

CHAPTER 3

Eventually Dari went back, he had to for himself. Mom was miserable without him, and it showed. He didn't want to but that was the only way he would get to see Luka. he was never worried about mom hurting him, neither was I. I just wanted him to come, even if mom would never hurt him, I knew she would scare him. I never really saw Dari after that. Mom would drop him off and pick him up at school on time every day. We were never around the same people so the only time I would see him is during passing period, and that was if I was lucky.

I would walk home with Alice every day. Often we would pass by mom's house. She always had friends over, even new ones. I saw her holding a man close to her, it wasn't Mr. Walker but it was someone. She was happy, but when I saw Dari, he wasn't. I wondered why, I needed to know why.

"Dari?"

"Jade? How are you? God, you have no idea how much I've missed you."

"What's wrong?"

"What do you mean?"

"You are always sad, what's wrong?"

"I just missed you and Mr. Walker fired mom because she got rid of you. Now I can't see Luka without them getting suspicious."

"I'm sorry Dari."

"No, it wasn't your fault, it was mom's she shouldn't have done that to you, none of that. You didn't deserve that."

"Thank you Dari, but I think I have a way for you to see Luka."

"How?"

"Meet me at Alice's house, now."

"Okay." He came, I knew he would. As soon as he saw me or I saw him he hugged me tight and cried in my shoulder.

"Oh my God, I missed you so much!"

"I missed you too brother." It felt nice to call him my brother, I was always used to calling him by his name it was different calling him brother. I looked him in the eye and grabbed his hand. I knew how to drive and Mrs. Lee

gave me the keys to her car, I could get in trouble for this

but so long as my brother is happy. I lead him to her car.

We both get in and I drive away.

"You know how to drive?"

"Mhmm."

"I did not see that coming."

"You know all sides to him."

"Who?"

"Luka."

"Oh, yeah."

"All sides?"

"Yes. what are you getting at?"

"I place I am taking you is where he spends most of his time, I want to make sure you know every side so I don't show you something you don't want to see."

"Don't worry, I know every side of him, I've slept with him so there is no side I haven't seen."

"I did not need to know that."

"You already knew."

"I did not need to be reminded."

I drove him to the one place where I know he always is. One place I used to go, times were dark then and I was reckless. Here they sold drugs, had sex with fuck boys and prostitutes, raced, and did whatever they pleased. I only watched, I never did anything like that. I hoped he had never been here, I hoped Luka never took Dari here.

I never wanted him to see these things. We both got out .
. . oh no. Dari saw it too, his face dropped. Luka was
kissing another guy, probably the same age as Dari. I
wanted to take him back but Dari was already running to
him.

"Luka?"

"Dari? What're you doing here?"

"I was going to surprise you but looks like your surprise
was good enough for me."

"I'm sorry Dari, there was no way you and I could see
each other, so I moved on."

"Yeah, I can see that! You moved on really quick didn't
you, not even a week!"

"Sorry Dari, that's just the way the world works."

Seeing my brother break like that hurt me a lot. Some of the people here were looking at me, they knew me and I knew them. They joined when I did. Some were old "friends" and some were old enemies. I never struck trouble but some people just didn't like me.

"Hey gang, look who's back. Jakie. Ha, miss us after four years?"

I hated that name, I had no idea why they always called me Jackie but they said I needed a street name so if I got famous people wouldn't know my real name and the police couldn't lock me up. I knew I would never get famous but they always hoped I would. Dari was already falling apart; I knew it but he wouldn't show it.

"Okay asshole, why don't you find yourself another twelve years old to fuck, that'll do you a lot better won't it?"

"Oh shit!"

"Damn, that boy got you good!"

"Shut up dickhead!" Dari walked away and so did I before anyone said anything else.

We drove away in silence, neither of us said a word. The only sounds heard were the hum of the car and Dari's short sniffles. I wanted to say something but I thought it would be better if I said nothing.

"I'm sorry, I didn't know."

"No, it's not your fault. I should've known he was using me. I just don't understand why, do you?"

"Yes."

"Why? And why did all those people know you? They called you Jackie."

"I know. When I was twelve, I came here looking for somewhere to go, somewhere to get away from mom. I thought I would fit in; I did in a way. Everybody there has a street name, to protect from the cops."

"Oh, but how did you know he was using me?"

"Because, I knew him before. I knew his reputation. I knew he slept with younger crowds, that's how he got popular. He would sleep with them then dump them. I tried to warn you but-"

"You did. You did try to warn me but I didn't listen. I thought he was different."

"I'm sorry."

"Why are you sorry?"

"Because I didn't warn you."

"You did, in the end, I'm the one at fault."

"No, in the end, he's the one at fault. He'll pay."

"How are you going to do that without getting me in trouble?"

"Don't worry, I won't involve that, I'll get him another way."

"Okay, I love you."

"I love you too."

After I dropped Dari off I went to Alice's house. I slept on one of the beds. After what seemed like a few hours, Alice woke me up.

"Hey, I didn't know you were back."

"Yeah, I got back a few hours ago."

"Okay, cool. My uncle's here talking with my mom."

"Huh? Why?"

"Don't know. But I think we are staying with him for a while."

"Why?"

"Your mom, she found out you took Dari somewhere and she's not happy. My mom told him everything. Since there is no longer any proof on you, if she does do anything, he can lock her up."

"But what about Dari?"

"He'll be fine, he'll come with us."

"Okay."

"Come on." I left with her and saw the two of them talking. When they saw us Mrs. Lee gave her usual worried look and Uncle Jacob his smile.

"Good evening ladies, how are we doing?"

"Good."

"That's great! Sorry to rain on your parade but unfortunately we've run into some bad news."

"What's that?"

"You can tell it to them straight Jacob, they're sixteen."

"Alright, alright. So, Jade your mom is upset because you

spent time with Dari yesterday, I'm not really sure why I

mean he is your brother but anyway, I found out from

Diana that she has been causing you some pain,

physically, is that true?"

I didn't really know what to say, if I said yes he'd ask for

proof or how she hurt me, my answers are always dull

and sometimes unbelievable so that's why most people

don't believe what I say, but if I say no, Mrs. Lee could

get in trouble for

"lying" and my mom could actually do something.

"Yes."

"She has?"

"Yes." "Have you told anyone." "No." "Then how did she find out?" "She guessed." "She guessed? How did she guess you were getting abused?"

"I don't know." "Jade, there are no wrong answers here, there is only the truth and you need to be telling me that." "Okay." "So, how did she guess you were being abused by your mother?" "The marks." "What marks?" "On me." "What kinds of marks?"

"Bruises, cuts." "I'm not saying you were but do you think it's possible you could have been doing this to yourself?" I have never thought of it that way, but it was possible people would think that. But I haven't, I'm not depressed, I have no reason to beat myself.

"Yes." "What?" "It's possible." "Okay, are you?" "No."

"So your mom has been beating you?" "Yes." "How? What has she done?" "It's like you don't believe her, Jacob."

"Look, I believe her but this is my job! I can't put her mom away just because she hates her! I want that woman put away just as much as you do but I can't just do it based off emotions!" "I don't." "I'm sorry?" "I don't hate her."

"That's good. I'm sorry, Jade, I really don't mean to be this way, I just have to do my job." "I understand."

"Okay, good. Now, how has she beat you."

"She throws things, and slaps me, and kicks me, and calls me names." "What things does she throw at you?" "Anything, shoes, bottles, rocks, anything."

"Okay, sorry to ask, but what did she call you?" "Isn't that enough?" "If she's stated it I need to ask it!" "I can't curse." "It's fine sweetheart, you have our permission."

"No, Uncle Jacob it's against our code."

"Oh, um, well can you write it? Is that alright?"

"That's fine." "Okay." I was given a pen and paper and wrote the words down. They were words I had heard so many times before, they meant nothing to me, they could not hurt me. Bitch . . . Whore . . . Asshole . . . Shithead . . . I gave it to him, they both read it. As they went down the list their expressions changed. Uncle Jacob looked at me and Mrs. Lee began to cry. He walked up to me and kneeled. He placed his hand on my shoulder.

"Is this . . . is this true?" I nodded in response.

"Oh, Jade I'm so sorry." He wraps his arms around me and holds me tight. "Well . . . is that enough to put her away?"

"Unfortunately that is only enough to get her to lose everything she has, but not enough to put her away."

"Are you serious Jacob? She beats her and calls her horrible names!" "There is no physical proof!" "I'm sure it's been seen at school!"

"And what if, they probably resolved it!"

"What about witnesses?"

"Witnesses?! If there were witnesses that would definitely work! The witness could support your testimony! Who's your witness?"

"Dari. My brother." "Did he see it happen?" "Not the entire thing but he witnessed a lot of them." "Did he here her words." "She would shout them aloud." "So yes. Okay, you said he watched them, why?" "Mom made him."

"Did he do anything to stop it." "He's only twelve, he was too young but his crying would make her stop." "Good enough. Alright, I think we can get her. Thank you Jade."

"Don't forget."

"Forget? Oh, yeah Jade would you like to live with me? Diana thinks it would be good on both ends." I really would like to. I've always liked him, when I came over. He reminded me of the father I never had. He was kind and loving. He understood me on a different level than Mr. Walker. He had seen all sides to me.

"Overall, it is your decision."

"No, I want to."

"You do?"

"Really?"

"Yes."

"Oh I'm so glad! I promise I'll be a good parent."

"Haha, Jacob don't worry, you are a great Uncle, you'll be a great parent!" "Thanks Diana." I was genuinely happy. I really did like him. I gave my best smile, which wasn't bad. Besides being sixteen, he easily picked me up and hugged me tight. I was happy. I looked down and saw Alice smiling. Happiness was against our code but I think it was time to break code and fix our ways. Our course we would stay the same.

We wouldn't change in high school, but home would be different. At the very least I felt this way and I hope she did too. I was packing to go to Jacob's house, he said calling him anything was okay, except officer or mister. I felt a tap on my shoulder, I turned around and saw it was Alice, she was smiling.

"I think we need to talk."

"I think so too."

"You first."

"Okay . . . I think we should break code."

"Oh thank God, I was hoping I wasn't the only one."

"Haha, yeah, but maybe, let's not change until junior year." "Sounds good. When I smiled yesterday, I felt so happy."

"Was the code holding you back?" "No, I made it. I don't remember what held me back. But it wasn't the code and it wasn't you." "Thank you, for being my friend."

"Too minds think alike."

"Hahaha!"

"Ahahah!" We finally smiled.

I was so happy. I heard a knock at the door and so did Alice.

"Come in!" But no one walked in. we opened the door and saw no one was there, but the knocking still continued, this time it was louder. I went to the front door and opened it, my mistake.

"You little shit, what did you do?!"

"What?'

"You sent the cops to my door! They took Dari away and now they are trying to arrest me! For hitting you which you know I didn't do!" Yes, she did but she was trying to change my mind, it wouldn't work.

"Liar. You did hit her, several times, and Dari knows it."

"Dari doesn't know a thing. He's scared as shit! What did you do to him?"

"Nothing, I did nothing."

"Now he doesn't have a home."

"Yes he does, and so does she." She spun around and behind her was standing Mr. Walker, angry.

"B-ben, I, it's not what it seems!"

"It's plenty. If they don't lock you up I will."

"What?!" "You heard me. Now I've heard it and so has this girl." "But, I did nothing wrong! She hurt Dari! She ruined my life!"

"She didn't ruin your life, you did." Right behind mom was a man I had not seen in over ten years. He had left with nothing to say. He left without looking back. Jade didn't think he'd remember her.

"Hello, Dad."

CHAPTER 4

"Casey, what are you doing here?"

"This man here told me what you had been doing."

"What have I been doing?"

"Don't lie to me, Bitch, you know exactly what you've been doing. You've been blaming my daughter that she was the reason I left. I left because you are a Psycho Bitch."

"What? I don't understand? Why would you say that?"

"Because, I'm not a liar like you, I tell the truth." "But I didn't lie! You left right after she was born; she was the reason!"

"No Bitch she isn't the reason. I left you because I was through, you raising a child one your own was karma enough for me, if I could've I would have taken her with me but that meant having ties with you and I didn't even want to see you."

"But, I loved you!"

"You were obsessed with any man you could get your hands on, even your boss but he knew better." I looked at Mr. Walker who was glaring at mom. He couldn't have known but then again he might have known. He always ignored her personal questions and every time she mentioned lunch he would change the subject. He didn't like her in that way, and now he didn't like her at all.

"Come on Sarah Evans." Uncle Jacob was standing right behind her with cuffs in his hands. He grabbed her hands and cuffed her. His deputy took her away, most likely to the police station. Dad turned around and shook Mr. Walker's and Uncle Jacob's hand.

"Thanks again, Ben."

"No problem Casey. Anything for you two." Dad knew Mr. Walker. Mr. Walker, walked up to me and gave me a hug, looking at me with bottle green eyes.

"It was great to meet you Miss Jade Evans. I'm glad to say you are safe and I will be seeing you more often now." "It was great to meet you as well Mr. Walker." I was still confused. Dad stared at me, he didn't move. "I'm sorry Jade, I should've came back for you. This was the best I could do." "What?" "Your father planned this. That's the reason I even hired that woman, so I could keep an eye on you." "Do you know Officer Lee?"

"No, but he did help put her away."

"I'm just glad she's where she belongs." "Jade, would you like to live with Dari and I?" I wanted to, but I looked at Uncle Jacob and his face dropped but he tried to smile his best. I did not know my father and I should get to know him. But I already promised Uncle Jacob I would stay with him, and I am always true to my word.

"No thank you."

"No? Where will you live?" "I already said I was living with someone." "Who?" "Officer Jacob." "The police man?" "Yes, I said I would before you came and I am always true to my word." "Alright then." "Can I visit?" "Of course you can." "Okay." Dad left with Mr.

Walker and I turned to Uncle Jacob. He lifted me and hugged me tight, and I hugged him back. "Aw, Jade you made me so happy! But I have to warn you I am not the best parent." "That's okay, you'll be better than mom." "Thank you. Now, is there anyone else you'd like to call me? Of course you can still call me Uncle Jacob but anything else is fine."

He was going to be like a parent to me but calling him dad would be betrayal to my biological father. I could call him dad in another language, that way it's special. I want to make this special, but not childish. "My Papa." "My Papa? Aww that's so sweet, okay!" "Okay, thank you again My Papa." "No problem Mija." That was Spanish for daughter, now my name is special. I went home with My Papa, his home was clean and big, not an apartment but a big house.

Two stories. Downstairs was the kitchen, family room, living room, dining room, and one bathroom. Upstairs was the master bedroom, two other bedrooms, office, bathroom and guest room. Outside was a pool in the backyard and a place to sit and lay down in grass. He looked at me with beautiful nut brown eyes. He was My Papa and I was his Mija.

"Okay, love, I want to set some things straight." Rules, I was used to this. "I obviously don't how this parents thing works but I know you will help me. But, you are to ask for selfish things and you are allowed to tell me things, anything's.

Anything troubling you I want you to tell me. I want to feel at home and I want you to be spoiled. I will take care of the rest." I was not expecting this, My Papa was kind and he was loving, I hope Dari is okay with dad.

My Papa let me decorate my room however I wanted, and he helped me. I didn't paint it black but instead a soft grey. I had a small bed so I could have a desk and shelves with books. I also put a chair and a rug and couch in my room. Sometimes I would visit my dad and Dari. I am not sure if Dari was better with Sarah or with our father.

Neither of us call her mother, we both agreed she didn't deserve that title. Her hearing is tomorrow; our dad is forcing us to go so we can watch her go to prison. We have to dress in proper attire, I wear a dress while dad and Dari wear suits.

My Papa works this case so he will be there during the hearing, then after I will stay at his work until his shift is over. We walk into the courtroom and sit in one of the right pews. Mrs. Lee and Alice sit behind us and two adults I have never seen before sit in the pews on the left side.

They are elder and dressed in formal attire, their faces show no emotion and they look nowhere but in front of them. I have seen them before but Dari has not. Dad has seen them, he knows them, he glares at them.

They are Sarah's parents. They don't like us; they don't know us. They don't see us. They never see us. They were our grandparents until the day they disowned their daughter and everything she owned. Her mother said I am the way I am because she did not teach me right, when Sarah refused to give us to her parents they cut off all ties with her, including her children. Sarah had a younger brother Jay Evans, he looked everything like Dari.

I have seen pictures, young pictures. Maybe he was twelve, Dari's age. A man walked into the courtroom and sat beside her parents, Jay. He was our uncle. He would sometimes visit us. At times he seemed like the only one who cared for Sarah, besides Dari. It's not that I didn't care for her, I did, but she never wanted me to. She wanted me to stay away from her.

Jay always took care of her, Jay always took care of me, and Jay always took care of Dari. Jay cared for everyone, he loved everyone. Jay always smiled, even at serious times Jay smiled. I don't know much about him.

Today, Jay was not smiling, he was not happy, he was

not Jay. Unlike his parents he looked around, he saw me

looking at him and he smiled. I smiled back. I could

smile now; I could be happy. Today I didn't know if I

was supposed to be happy or not. Sarah was going to jail,

should I be happy she won't hurt me anymore or should I

be sad because I know she won't be safe in jail? I wasn't

living with her anymore so she couldn't hurt me, My

Papa wouldn't let her. I know she wasn't strong enough

to go to prison, she wasn't.

I heard Dari ask dad a question. "Does she have to go to

jail?" "Of course she does." "Why?" "She hurt your

sister?" "Can't you just, like, fine her or something like

that?"

"This is serious Dari, she abused your sister, don't you want your sister to get justice?" "Since when do you care? We've only known you a few days, you barely know us." "And that's where you're wrong, I know everything about you, it's you who knows nothing about me." "And we should trust you, why?" "Dari, this is not the place for that. You want to talk at home, fine, here we are quiet." "Why?" "Dari, shut it." "That doesn't answer my question."

"I'm not fooling around." "Neither am I." The courtroom doors open and walk in Mr. Walker and his son Luka. Dari sees him and almost immediately quiets down. Dad doesn't notice but I do, I notice because I know the truth. I watch Dari's every movement, from his rising glare to his way he digs his nails into his skin. Dad still does not notice, he never will. He will never notice the small things; he will never notice when something is troubling Dari because he doesn't know him. And no one except Alice, Dari, and My Papa will notice when something is troubling me, even Mr. Walker won't notice.

"Can Dari and I go for a walk?" "Why?" No answer I have no reason to answer him, he wouldn't understand anyway. "Fine, but be quick." We take Dari's hand and lead him out of the pew. We walk down the aisle and without turning I can see Luka glance at Dari. He knows he made a mistake. There is nothing he can do now because now Dari will never forgive him. I lead him outside the courthouse and we sit on the front steps. I stare at his hands.

He's bleeding. I reach for his hand but he pulls away.

"I'm sorry." "Why is he here?" "Because Mr. Walker

was dad's friend, he helped look after us. You know the

rest." "I know, I just wish Luka wasn't here too." "Me

too." "Jade," "Yes?" "Why is Sarah going to jail? And

why is dad happy about that? I mean I know she hurt

you, but why does she have to go to jail?" "Because she

broke the law. Abusing children or anyone under

eighteen is illegal and you can go to jail for it." "For how

long?" "I'm not sure." "Why is dad happy about that?" "I

don't know."

Okay. I do want you to get your justice, I just don't think

this is the way. Do you want her to go to jail too?

"No."

"You don't? But she hurt you." "I know, but wishing pain on those who have pained me does not make the pain hurt any less." "So in other words, putting her in jail won't get you your justice?" "I have no justice in putting her in jail." "You want her dead?" "No." "Why will putting her in jail not bring you justice?" "Because she'll learn nothing. My justice is not served because there is no justice to serve. My only wish is that she sees her wrong in what she did." "Do you think she will?" "It's not likely." "Oh, okay."

"Are you alright?" "I'll be fine." "Okay, let's go back." We walk back inside the courtroom and stand next to dad. My Papa is in front in uniform, standing next to the judge's bench. In his hand is a bible. I know what they do in hearings, I know how this goes. I'm ready.

Soon the hearing begins. We are all told to rise as the judge walks in, a woman. Then we are told to be seated. The jury sits in their box to the right and the plaintiff, dad's lawyer, and dad sit at their table while Sarah's lawyer and the defendant, Sarah, sit at the other table to the left.

The judge asks, "does the defendant plead guilty or not guilty to the charges." I have a faint hope she will plead guilty, if she does the hearing is over and she receives her sentence. If she pleads not guilty, the case will go on another day.

"Not guilty, your honor." I knew it. She wouldn't tell the truth, I hear faint murmurs from the jury and from the pews. The judge bangs his gavel and the room quiets down. "You, Sarah Evans, plead not guilty to the charges that were pressed against you for . . . for physically and verbally abusing your sixteen-year-old daughter?"

"Yes your honor." "Alright, the trial will be set three days from now, is that clear Mr. Lee?" "Yes your honor." "Good, dismissed." Everyone gets up and Sarah is taken away. Dad talks with his lawyer, he's angry. The lawyer tells him to say nothing, nothing that will risk losing the case. Dari and I wait outside the courtroom on the benches.

People pass us by, cops and cops with criminals, family members and lawyers. I hear footsteps growing louder and I look up to face Jay and his parents. Jay kneels down and smiles at me, while his parents stay the same. "Hey Angel, how you doing?" "Fine." "That's good. So, in case your mother does go to jail, we would love for the

both of you to live with us." "We're okay." "What?"
"We've already got places to live." "If you think you are staying with your idiotic father you can think again." I look up and his mother, they both are glaring at us while Jay looks confused.

"Wait, you said places, are you not living in the same places?" "No, Dari lives with dad and I live with my friend's uncle." "Why?"

"It doesn't matter; they are living with us." "No, we are not." "What did you say little girl?" "We already have places to live, we are fine."

"I don't care, from now on you are living with us." "No." "You can't say no so get into the car, we are going home." "No, why do you care now?"

"What?" "Why do you care now? You disowned your daughter and everything she owned so why do you care now?" "What? This is unbelievable! I am not leaving you with that man and that is final!" "No, we are staying where we are."

"Jade, please rethink this." "No, we are staying." "No. You. Are. Not." "Is there a problem here?" My Papa was standing in between us and them. I'm glad he is here now I can go with him.

"No, not at all officer." "Alright then, let's not shout in the hall." "Okay." Dad walks out the door with Mr. Walker and Luka.

I look at Dari but he is staring at the ground. I feel a hand on my shoulder and look up. My Papa looks at me and I look at him. "Ready to go?" I know their eyes widen, Jay and his parents are surprised. I am ready to go but I don't want to leave Dari.

I look at Dari and he smiles. I know he will be alright, I look at My Papa and I nod. "Yes, I'm ready." "Okay, let's go." I walk with him to his car and we drive to the station. There I sit at his desk and wait for his shift to end. Many things happen at the station. Many bad news is told, many criminals are brought in and cops are everywhere.

One cop throws a man down on his chair and tells him to stay put. If he's smart he'll stay put, this area is filled with cops. He is semi-smart. He turns towards me and looks up and down, licking his lips. "Hey baby girl, how you doing'?" I ignore him. "Oh, so you the quiet type, huh? That's' okay, I get it. No problem, we all good.

Hey, you want to help me out of this? Help me, and I'll help you, how's that sound, huh?" I ignore him.

"Ah, come on baby g-" "Is there a problem buddy?" My Papa is here, thank god. "No problem at all officer."

"Then why were you talking to my daughter?"

His eyes go wide. "Oh, now you see, I don't know she was your daughter, I just thought she was . . . uh . . ." "Yeah, save it for later buddy." I can hear him mutter "damn cops" under his breath, and so does My Papa.

"What was that?" "Nothing." "No, you got something to say don't you?" "What's the problem here Lee?" "I think your boy has something he'd like to say." "Oh really, and what would that be? You think you a tough guy huh?"

"Nah man, I say nothing." "I think you did so why don't you just say it again?" No answer. "That's what I thought." The officer takes him away and the day continues.

A few hours pass and his shift ends. My Papa looks exhausted, we walk to the car but he looks too tired to drive. I offer to drive, since I can. He lets me drive and I take us home. A few minutes later we are at home and he goes to bed while I go to my room. I look at my phone and I have over twenty texts, all from Dari.

MR. WALKER AND LUKA ARE AT THE HOUSE. LUKA WON'T STOP STARING AT ME. I WENT TO MY ROOM AND HE FOLLOWED ME HERE, I HAD TO GO INTO THE BATHROOM TO GET AWAY FROM HIM. HE WON'T LEAVE ME ALONE! JADE I

NEED YOU RIGHT NOW MORE THAN EVER PLEASE, HELP ME! That last text was sent only three minutes ago, I wake up My Papa and ask him if I can go visit Dari, he says I can but to be back before eleven.

He also gives me money to eat since neither of us had eaten all day. I drive to dad's house and Dari is outside, he gets into the car and we drive away. I park the car in the parking lot of our favorite restaurant, Wood Ranch. I look at Dari, he's on the verge of tears.

"You want to tell me what happened?"

"Yes . . ."

CHAPTER 5

I let Dari gather himself before he began, he was still crying when he began his story. "So, what happened?"

"Well . . . I was in the living room sitting on the couch while dad, Mr. Walker and Luka were in the kitchen. I was just on my phone texting you when he sat next to me on the couch. I tried to move away but he put his arm around me. I asked him what he was doing and he leaned into me and whispered in my ear that they didn't know we weren't friends anymore. He told me to also act kindly for him."

"Did you?"

"Hell no! I pushed away and went into my room, he still followed me. He kept talking to me saying all kinds of things but the one thing I didn't hear him say was "sorry".

He never apologized for what he did! He had the nerve to do everything else except apologize! I was so mad I went into the bathroom but he followed me in there. He grabbed me by hair and dragged me to my bed. He climbed on top of me and covered my mouth with tape. He said to not scream or he'll make it worse. He tied my hands above my head and started taking off his clothes . . . and then mine . . . ." He began crying again, I put my hand on his back and he leaned into me.

I held him there, trying to calm him down, eventually it worked. "He did the same thing we did over and over again, multiple times so we didn't feel the same? I kept trying to scream but the tape was still over my mouth, it hurt so bad."

"He raped you."

"He what?" "He raped you. He forced you to have sex with him even when you didn't want to." "I thought it was something different, Sarah said that rape was someone forcing themselves on you but you say no."

"It's the same thing, but you couldn't, you had tape over your mouth. You didn't want it to happen, did you?"

"No! I never want it to happen again!" I let him talk and then we got dinner, we had enough but it was already past eleven o'clock. I looked at my phone, three missed calls from My Papa. He must be worried, but I can't leave Dari at that house. I think of a plan. I drive him home and tell him to stay in the car. I knock on the door and dad answers, he's angry.

"Jade? Where the hell is Dari? We've been looking for him for the past two hours!" "He's with me." "WHAT?! What the hell do you mean?!" "He's with me, we went out for dinner." "Well where is he now?!" "He wants to stay over with me. I'm here to get his stuff." "Hell no, he's grounded! Where is he?"

"Sleeping."

"Where Jade?" "I don't want to wake him up.

"Fine then, I will." "You can't." "Why?!" "Because, he's already at my house." "I thought you said he was with you."

"He was." "Well bring him back, he's grounded."

"He wants to stay with me, I'll bring him to school tomorrow." "No, absolutely not, bring his ass back here."

"Careful Casey, you know who's on the line here."

"That kid didn't tell me he was going anywhere; I'm worrying over here while he's having a hell a good time!" "Calm down." "Fine!" "You know, Jade, the least he could've done was tell me he was going." "He's only twelve, he didn't know. Unless you told him and he forgot." "He should know! His damn mother near locked him in a closet his whole life!"

"Exactly, she went everywhere with him so there was no need to tell her he was going anywhere. He couldn't."

"Makes sense I guess, just make sure you tell him he has to tell me next time and not just run off, okay?" "Okay."

"Okay, thank you. No go on and get his things."

"Okay." I walk off to his room and get some things he'll need; things he'll always need. I'm almost done when I hear footsteps, I turn around and Luka is standing in the doorway blocking my path. "Did he tell you what happened?"

"What happened?"

"I know you know, Jade. I'm not stupid." "Yes, you are." "What?" "You should have known better than to touch him."

"He wanted me to, what could I do?" "Today? He wanted you today? I think not." "Well I'm sorry, I couldn't help myself." "Stay away from him." "And how exactly are you going to explain to our dads that we aren't friends anymore?" "There's no need.

Mr. Walker wanting to know us was all a part of dad's plan to make sure we were safe. You being friends with Dari was all a part of the plan as well." "Not to Dari. To Dari I was his lover. I was his everything." "Not anymore." "And why is that?" "You should know." "Dari never knew about that place; I never took him there. You wanted to expose me, you never liked me at all."

"I have nothing towards you." "What?" "I don't care for you; you mean nothing to me." "You knew everything about me, you knew that I was doing it behind his back." "No, I didn't. That I was unaware of but I had a feeling you would stoop down to that level."

"What level?" "The level of a fuck boy." "You little bitch. You know me. I am not a fuck boy." "You have sex with twelve-year-old boys. You use them for your own personal gain." "So what? I like sex. What's wrong with that?"

"But the pieces together and you'll find your answer." "I like sex with twelve-year-old boys, so what? I like the way they scream for more." "You're disgusting." "And you're no different." "I'm not like you." "Maybe not, but I think I have a new type." "No." "Yup, the quiet ones. You know the quiet ones are the most dangerous." A term I've heard all my life. And I believe it, but not like that. "I agree, so back off." "Oh, you're an aggressive one?"

"You have a sex addiction and you need help." "Nah, I don't need help. I need you." "No." "Why not?" "No, I'm telling you no. If you don't listen, you're going to jail."

"If I go to jail, I'm telling all. Everything. Then Dari will get in trouble. You don't want that do you?" "Dari won't get in trouble. He didn't know it was wrong. And if Dari goes there are no limits to what he'll say." "What do you mean?" "He'll tell the cops about you and your little gang." "And you? You were there too."

"He doesn't know that." "Then I'll tell." "I didn't do anything illegal, I didn't drink, I didn't pay for sex and I didn't get paid. I was there and that was all."

"I don't care. So lay down and be a good girl." He leans in to kiss me so I kick him in the crotch. I run out the door, leaving him in pain. I get into the car and drive away. "What took you so long?" "Never mind that, I'll tell you later." We got home and My Papa rushed to hug me, he wasn't mad. He was only worried. I told him Dari wanted to stay over but I didn't tell him why, I have to be careful, I have to make sure Dari knows. "Dari, do you know what you did with Luka was wrong?"

"Well, I knew Sarah wouldn't like it." "Yes, she wouldn't have liked it. But what you were doing was also illegal." "Wait, illegal? You mean, I can go to jail?" "Depends, did you know that was wrong?" "No, I just thought that Sarah didn't like it. Did you know?" "Yes." "Why didn't you tell me?" "You wouldn't listen." "I guess you're right, but Jade I don't want to go to jail." "And you won't. You didn't know."

"Did Luka know." "Yes, he did." "That Bastard!" "Do you know how I knew he would be there?" "You've been there before?" "Yes, I have. And it was illegal. I should not have been there." "Oh, but you didn't know." "I did."

"Will you go to jail?" "No, I did nothing wrong." "Will you tell Officer Lee?" My Papa. If I told him he would never look at me the same. But I have to, but I can't tell Dari that. I have to tell My Papa the truth, everything. After Dari fell asleep I went into My Papa's room. He was awake, I sat on his bed and he pulled me into his arms.

He often did this when we watched movies on the couch. "Can I tell you something?" "Of course mija. What's on your mind?" "You won't like it." "What's wrong?" "You won't like me after." "No, mija, nothing you say or do or anyone, could ever make me love you less." "Okay . . ." I tell him everything. About Dari and Luka, I told him Dari didn't know. I told him about me and the place I visited. I told him I did nothing wrong.

I told him what Luka did and what he tried to do again. I also told him what Dari said and what Luka said. I told him everything. When I was done, he looked at me with the same look he gave me always. He smiled. "Now you know the truth, I'm sorry." "Oh Mija, there is no reason to be sorry. You told me the truth and that makes me happy.

Now Luka is seventeen and Dari is twelve so there isn't much we can do about that. But, he did rape him and he tried with you, that I can work with. And don't worry, you weren't in your right mind set when you were there, hell if I was treated the way you were I'd probably be there myself. So long as you did nothing you'll be fine. Now, I'll probably have to ask you and Dari to come to the station, but you have school tomorrow.

I also don't think bringing this up will be a good idea with the upcoming case involving your mother. I'll let my boss know tomorrow. Okay Mija, time for you to go to bed. Night." He kisses the top of my head and gives me one last hug before I go. I tell him goodnight and climb into my bed. Dari is also in my bed; I couldn't let him sleep on the floor.

He hugs me and I hug him, I have no idea what will happen tomorrow but I'm just hoping it will be good. My Papa drives Dari and me to school. I see Luka when I walk to my first period class, i hope he doesn't think anything will come of this. I decide it is only fair that I give him a warning, one that will take him awhile to understand, that way I can say I did warn him.

During my free period I read my book. He and three of his friends have free period last as well. I have to stay after school so I can pick up Dari and walk with Alice. He and his friends are walking to the front gate. They stop by the tables where I sit.

"Hey Jade, you want to walk with us baby girl?" No, I don't but I'll leave and wait in the coffee shop for both Alice and Dari. I get up and stop right by him.

"Even the quiet ones are never silenced." And then I walk out the gates, and I don't look back.

CHAPTER 6

I wait for them in the coffee shop, they run up to me looking scared.

"Jade?! What happened? You weren't at the school!"

"We got news from Luka that you left." "Why does he know that?"

"He saw me at the tables, we both have free period for our last class."

"What did he say to you?!" "He asked me if I wanted to walk with him."

"What did you say?" I could never tell them what happened, what I said, everything would be destroyed if I did.

"Nothing, I walked away."

"Good."

"Okay . . . are you okay?" "I'm fine." I knew he didn't believe me, but I was telling the truth. I was fine. We left to My Papa's house, Alice went to her own. I thought I should take Dari back, but he didn't want to. Anyways I took him, Luka was there. He definitely did not want to go. I walked him there, I knocked on the door and Luka answered. "Well, well, well. Look who it is."

"Where is our dad?"

They aren't home, my dad made me stay back just in case Dari might come back. And look who was right."

"Are you going to be okay?"

"I'll be fine." "Okay." Dari walks into his room. Luka stares at me, I turn to leave but he grabs my arm. "Wait a second, what did you mean by what you said earlier?"

"You'll find out soon enough."

"What? What do you mean?"

"You'll find out soon enough." "Oh, so you think I'm stupid, huh? I know you told that cop." No answer. "You're going to pay for that, Love. I'll tell him everything." "I already did." "You even told him that Dari and I had sex."

"Yes." "No you didn't, you wouldn't. You're lying."

"Okay."

"Whatever, you're going to pay. I can promise you that."

"Okay."

I leave for my house, I know he won't touch Dari,

because if he does Dari will tell. I get there and My Papa

greets me with a kiss on the cheek and a hug. He has to

leave for work tonight, I know that. I go to my room and

lay on my bed and I think, think of how My Papa will

handle this.

Wondering if Dari will get into trouble? Wondering if I

will as well? I don't know but this isn't something I

should worry about, since either way it is out of my

control, for now. I nap after doing homework, though I

don't ever have dreams.

I'm not sure why dreams don't occur in my mind, though

nightmares appear more often than I would like. I was in

a car but I was not driving, I was in the back seat. I

looked to the front I saw a person; someone I didn't recognize.

"Hello?"

"Don't worry love they won't ever take you away from me again." "Huh? What? Who are you?" "You don't remember me?"

"No." "I didn't think you'd ever forget." "I'm sorry." I didn't know but his voice was familiar. "Where are you taking me?" "Home." "Where is home?"

"You'll see." Then suddenly someone appeared in the passenger seat next to the mystery man. "Who are you?"

"You 'll find out soon enough."

"I don't understand." "Quiet now." "But-" I suddenly went silent. I touched where tape was covering my mouth. I wanted to scream but I was mute or no one could hear me. I felt something bump my leg. I looked down at a large black blanket. I moved it and was My Papa tied up with tape covering his mouth. He was covered in blood and I didn't know if this was still a dream. I looked right and saw my brother tied up with a knife sticking out of his stomach.

I reached to touch him as he was cold, dead. What was happening?! I looked up as the car pulled up into a driveway, Alice's house. I didn't know what to do so I tried to scream, forgetting about the tape silencing me. The mystery man got out of the car and opened the door.

I tried to look at his face but his face was covered in black. He grabbed My Papa and then the second man grabbed me.

They both draped us over their shoulders. I tried to move

but I couldn't, suddenly my hands were tied to my body.

They opened the door and I saw my three friends. Alice,

Mrs. Lee and Mr. Walker were all on the floor covered in

blood, dead. No, no, no, no, no, this can't be, this can't

be happening.

"And you're next . . ."

I tried to scream, they were coming at me with a knife.

My Papa screamed and kicked.

"Don't worry, you'll get yours soon enough." I screamed

as the knife entered my gut, as I felt everything go numb.

My Papa screamed until the man pulled out a gun, black.

"Now how does it feel to be at the other end? Bon

Voyage, Bastard."

BAM! BAM! BAM!

"NO!"

"Baby what's wrong?!" I looked up and saw My Papa

staring into my eyes with fright.

"You, you Were-I-he-"

"No, no, no baby doesn't worry about it. You just had a

nightmare." Yes, I did, but my nightmares were never

this vivid. I was terrified but not for myself, for my

family. And even now I still don't know who those men

were.

I try to close my eyes and look back at them. Nothing,

they were both covered in black, but one was taller than

the other. Today I live in fear and I show it more than I'd

like to but my nightmares are never there just to frighten

me, they always mean something. And I am praying to

God that my nightmare won't come true.

CHAPTER 7

The trial got held back three days because the judge had business to attend and all other judges already had cases to attend. But when the trial came, all secrets broke loose. I watched them bring Sarah into the courtroom in chains.

She showed no emotion whatsoever. The judge entered and everyone stood up. Dari wasn't next to me and My Papa was not in the room, instead a different officer took his place. My father stood tall next to me thinking he'd get justice but what justice was he receiving? His ex-wife was being put away for sure unless she could prove she did nothing, which wasn't likely. And soon enough, the trial began . . .

"You, Sarah Evans, have pleaded not guilty in the abuse of your daughter."

"Yes, your honor."

"And you realize if you are proved wrong you will be sentenced to a lifetime in prison."

"Yes, your honor."

"Alright, then let the trial begin." And so it went, there were pictures of the cuts and bruises on my body, everywhere. And I told my part.

"Jade, how old are you?"

"Sixteen." "And how long has your mom been abusing you?"

"All my life."

"Can you be sure of this?" "Yes."

"How?" "She would always do it, she would always tell

me things as well, things only my mom could know."

"What kinds of things did she do?"

"She would throw things at me, and she would kick me

and scream things at me."

"What things would she scream at you?"

"That I ruined her life, that I'm the reason her life is so

terrible, that . . ."

"What?"

"Miss Evans you must answer the question."

"She one night told me I'm the reason my dad left."

I looked down at my lap too afraid to look my dad in the eyes, but I knew he was staring at me.

"And you're sure of this?"

"Yes."

"How many times has she told you this."

"Once."

"Can you recall when?"

"No." It's not as much that as it is I don't want to.

"Has she ever hurt your brother?"

"No."

"Are you certain."

"Yes."

"How so?"

"I knew."

"How could you know?"

"He would tell me if something happened."

"Did he?"

"No."

"No further questions your honor."

"Alright, Miss Evans you may return to your seat now."

"Thank you."

As I walked back to my seat I could feel my mother's glare on me, next up they called my father.

"Mr. Evans, how long have you known your daughter?"

"What do you mean?"

"How long have you known of your daughter's existence?"

"All her life, why would you ask that?"

"Did you leave before or after her birth?"

"Before."

"Why?"

"Because I didn't want to be stuck with that woman any longer. I knew as soon as a child was in the picture, I would never be able to leave without that guilt tying me down."

"But you knew of the child? Surely you knew you'd be leaving them behind, what was the difference in leaving before or after.

All it meant was you were leaving this poor mother to

raise a child on her own, two children in fact."

"Yes I knew of the child, but I found it better that I was

not engraved in their memory. The difference was

whether or not I would want to be in the picture or not.

Poor mother? Ha! This "poor mother" abused her

daughter for years! And I left her everything! How do

you call that poor?" "She had no one to help her."

"She had friends that she lied to that could help her!"

"Lied to?"

"She never told them that Jade was her daughter,

everyone thought she was a maid, as she treated her like

a slave."

"I did not! I was left with her! She was able to work so I put her to work, what's so wrong with that?!" "Mrs. Evans keep your voice down!"

"It isn't true!"

"Yes it is! I didn't want to be around you but I knew my daughter was being abused! I saw her walking down the street one day and I didn't even recognize her, and I had seen her multiple times before, she had a black eye and cuts and bruises everywhere! I don't think it's possible to do all that to yourself! So I asked my friend to keep an eye on her to make sure she was okay! And clearly she wasn't! Call me crazy but I never left my daughter and I damn well never left because of her, I left because of you!"

"That is enough! We will take a fifteen-minute break."

I exited and found Dari at the back with our grandparents and Jay surrounding him.

"Everything's going to be okay, you'll come home with us."

"Dari?"

"Jade!!" Dari ran over to me and hugged me tight. And I held him close.

"Is it over? Is mom gone?"

"No, not yet, we had to take a break."

"Hey kiddo, how are you?"

"I'm fine."

"You sure?"

"Yes." I still had no idea where My Papa was. I spent the entire break with Dari, and I told him everything.

"You told him? What will he do? Will we get into trouble?"

"No, we shouldn't."

"You're sure?"

"No, but I promise everything will be fine, do you trust me?"

"Of course I do, you're my sister."

"Good." The break ended and this time both Dari and I entered. Turns out the jury had enough evidence to make a decision. "How do you find the defendant, Sarah Evans?"

"We find the defendant guilty, your honor." "Sarah Evans you have been found guilty and sentenced to a lifetime in prison."

"No! Please! This isn't fair! Please!" She pleaded as she left the room, crying that this was unfair and maybe it was, maybe she didn't deserve to go to jail. That's one thing I'll never know. As soon as we were about to exit My Papa came in the courtroom.

"You honor, wait!"

"What is it Officer Lee?"

"Our second case."

"Ah yes, Benjamin Walker, Luka Walker, Jade Evans, Dari Evans and Casey Evans, hold back for a minute." I walked over and My Papa wrapped his arms around me and whispered in my ear. "Everything's going to be okay."

"Mr. Walker do you understand why you and your son have been called in here?" "No, your honor, i don't."

"Well I've been told that your son, Luka, has been having sex with Mr. Evans' son Dari. and you realize that it is illegal for your son who is now eighteen to be having sex with a twelve-year-old." "Luka is this true?" "Yeah but I didn't force it on him, he asked for it, I didn't think that was wrong." "Regardless you were having sex with a little boy."

"It doesn't matter who wanted it, he is under age, you should have known better that it was illegal." "Well I didn't."

"I also see that Dari isn't the only one he's been doing this with."

"Luka!" He had no words. "There is no need for a trial since you have confessed to it, I am sentencing you to six months in prison with a bail of $100,000, officers?" They took Luka away, most likely to the same place Sarah was going.

My father and Mr. Walker were confused so I told them everything, and Dari confessed as well. Because he didn't know it was wrong and he is underage they decided to give him a warning instead of sending him to juvie. Mr. Walker wasn't angry at us but he was disappointed in his son, and our father couldn't say much because he wasn't there.

"I just can't believe Luka would do something like that. I'm so sorry Dari and Jade."

"It's okay, I'm sorry. Maybe had I known he wouldn't have gone to jail."

"It's not your fault, he should've known better, he was older.'

"And I'm sorry, I didn't know what else to do."

"No jade, don't be sorry, my son threatened you like that you had every right, don't worry. You did the right thing."

"Are you going to bail him out?"

"Maybe in a few months, he won't learn anything if he doesn't stay there for at least a few months." "Do you think he'll be angry?"

"I don't care, what he did was wrong, this is nothing more than the punishment he deserved. Anyways, I'm glad you both are okay, bye for now."

"Bye." Dari safely went home with our father and I went home with My Papa, they gave him the rest of the day off.

"So, how are you feeling?"

"I'm okay, glad it's over and the truth is out."

"That's great. Well, what do you want to do? Go out to eat? See a movie? The mall? Whatever you want to do Love, I'm here for you."

"Thank you, but it's been a long day, I would actually like to go home."

"Great choice, let's go home."

www.ingramcontent.com/pod-product-compliance
Lightning Source LLC
Chambersburg PA
CBHW070532160726

48003CB00004B/1765